Easy micro:bit Projects

Eric Hagan

Maker Media, Inc.

San Francisco

C334477735

Easy micro:bit Projects
Eric Hagan

Published by Maker Media, Inc., 1700 Montgomery Street, Suite 240, San Francisco, CA 94111

Maker Media books may be purchased for educational, business, or sales promotional use. Online editions are also available for most titles (safaribooksonline.com). For more information, contact our corporate/institutional sales department: 800-998-9938 or corporate@oreilly.com. Customers may purchase kits, books, and more directly from us at Maker Shed.

ISBN: 9781680455540

Publisher: Roger Stewart
Illustration and Design: Eric Hagan
Editor: Patrick Di Justo
Cover Design: Juliann Brown and Julie Cohen

The author would like to thank his wife Marie Pantojan for all of her support and advice, and his colleague Jody Culkin for suggesting this idea in the first place.

Introducing the micro:bit!

Let's start by getting familiar with the **BBC micro:bit**, a miniature and powerful microcontroller which can be used as the basis of a number of exciting electronics projects. Some projects we plan to build in this book include:

Wayfind Plus, a high tech compass to point you in the right direction.

Tilt! a handheld tilt game which **plays music when you lose** and **saves your high score!**

The **Wave-o-tron,** an electronic musical instrument **controlled by waving your hands.**

A Four Wheeled robot that can sense and avoid obstacles.

A digital plant monitoring system which alerts you when you need to water your plants.

The electronics parts you will need to complete all ten projects are included on a list located on Page **53.** You will also need some additional tools and materials which you can find at a hardware or craft supply store.

A few tools we will need:

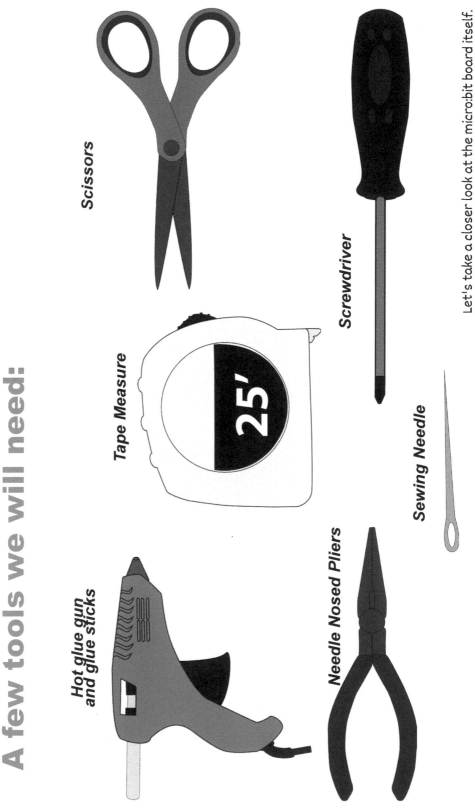

Hot glue gun and glue sticks

Tape Measure

Scissors

Needle Nosed Pliers

Sewing Needle

Screwdriver

Let's take a closer look at the micro:bit board itself.

micro:bit from front to back

The front of the micro:bit contains a **5x5 LED grid**, two Programmable **Push Buttons**, three labeled digital or analog input/output rings, and connection points for **3** volt power and ground.

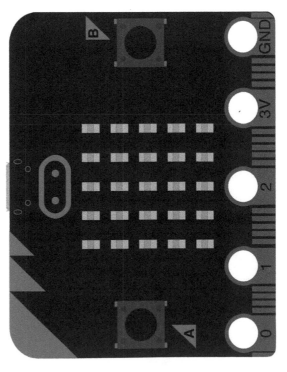

The back of the micro:bit contains the MicroUSB port, a reset button, the battery connector, the Bluetooth antenna, the processor, the compass, the accelerometer, and twenty edge pin connectors.

We will use most of these parts in our upcoming projects, but don't worry about memorizing where everything is, as you will be seeing these diagrams again.

Project 1
Making a scrolling name tag

We are going to start by creating a **scrolling text marquee** like those seen in a shop window. We will start by writing out the sentence "Hi, my name is" and your name. This project works by turning on and off LEDs in the grid on the front face of the micro:bit in to simulate moving text. This first project will help you feel comfortable programming and loading your projects onto the micro:bit.

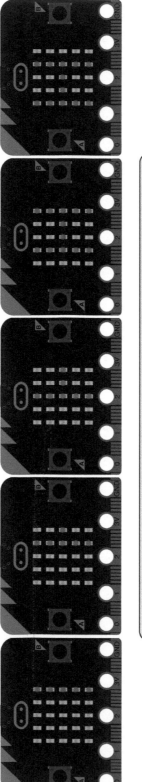

It takes five frames (images) to have the letter H scroll onto the screen. The last frame shows the 'H' in its final place. That's just the first letter of our text!

CAUTION

DO NOT unplug your microbit while you are uploading code as it could corrupt your program!

while there are several options for coding the micro:bit, we will be using the **Javascript Blocks editor** (powered by MakeCode) for most of our projects. The code editor is available for free on the web at **https://makecode.microbit.org**. Let's take a look at the code editor in a web browser:

Javascript Blocks Editor in your web browser

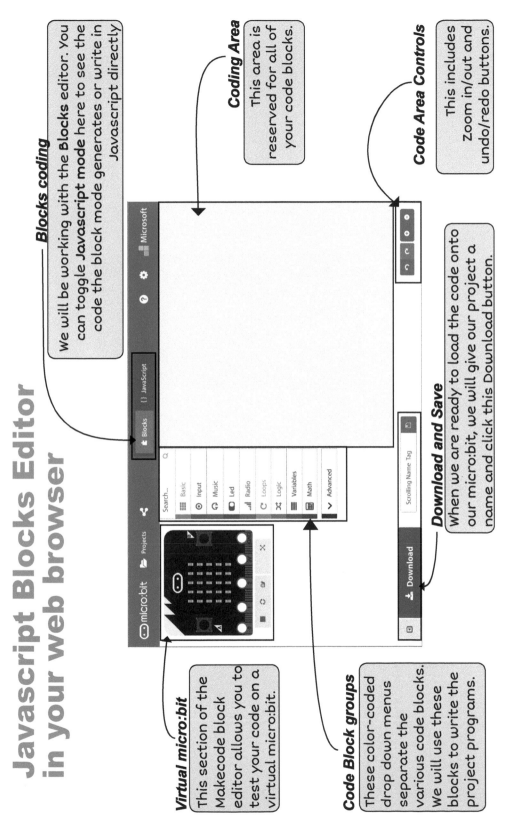

Blocks coding

We will be working with the **Blocks** editor. You can toggle **Javascript** mode here to see the code the block mode generates or write in Javascript directly

Coding Area

This area is reserved for all of your code blocks.

Code Area Controls

This includes zoom in/out and undo/redo buttons.

Virtual micro:bit

This section of the Makecode block editor allows you to test your code on a virtual micro:bit.

Code Block groups

These color-coded drop down menus separate the various code blocks. We will use these blocks to write the project programs.

Download and Save

When we are ready to load the code onto our micro:bit, we will give our project a name and click this Download button.

Basic coding for Project 1

When you create a new code project, the code blocks for on start and forever are automatically included.

On start
Code blocks attached to on start runs exactly once when the micro:bit is turned on or reset.

Forever
Code blocks attached to forever will repeat over and over until the micro:bit is powered down or reset.

1 Click on the Basic code block and a pop open menu will appear.

We need to drag the show string code block to our coding area. We want the name tag to loop, so we will add it to the forever code.

2 Attach the show string block by dragging it into the forever block, and then replace the text with "Hi, my name is " and your name.

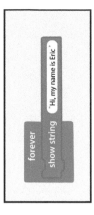

That's it! We have now finished all of the code we need for the first project. Our next step is to upload it to your micro:bit.

Loading your project onto the micro:bit

1 Now that the code is finished, input the project name "scrolling name tag" into the text box at the bottom of the code editor, and then hit the download button

Scrolling Name Tag

⬇ Download

2 Your web browser will save a .hex file named *microbit-Scrolling-name-tag.hex* in the default download location on your computer. This is generally the "Downloads" folder. Open this folder.

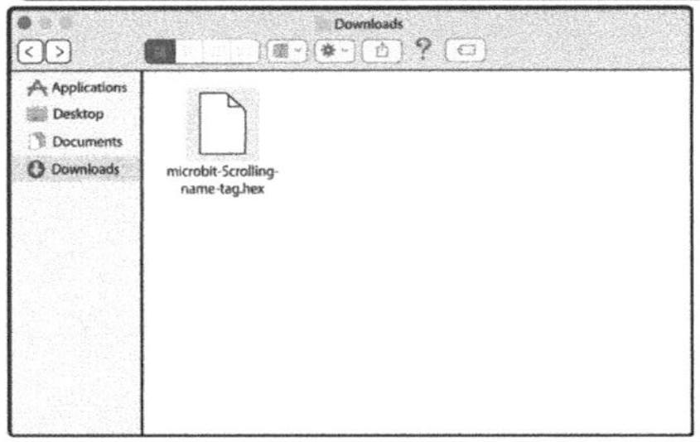

microbit-Scrolling-
name tag.hex

3 Plug your micro:bit into your computer using the *microUSB* cable. Any availabe USB port should be fine. The micro:bit will show up on your computer as a USB drive with the name "MICROBIT."

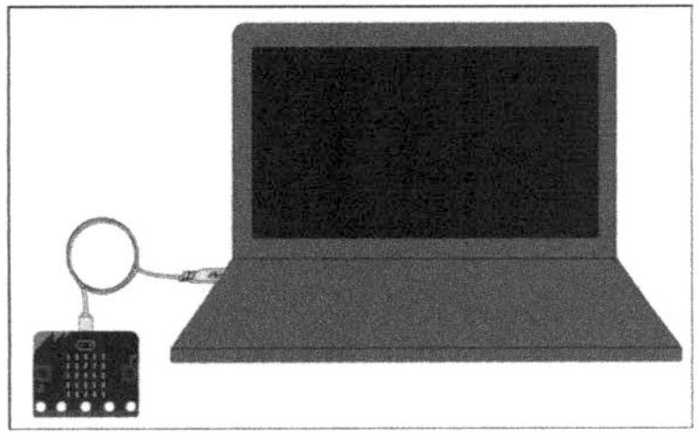

4 Drag the hex file from your desktop to the *MICROBIT drive*. The yellow power light on the back of your micro:bit will flash. Now your code is uploaded and your name tag will run!

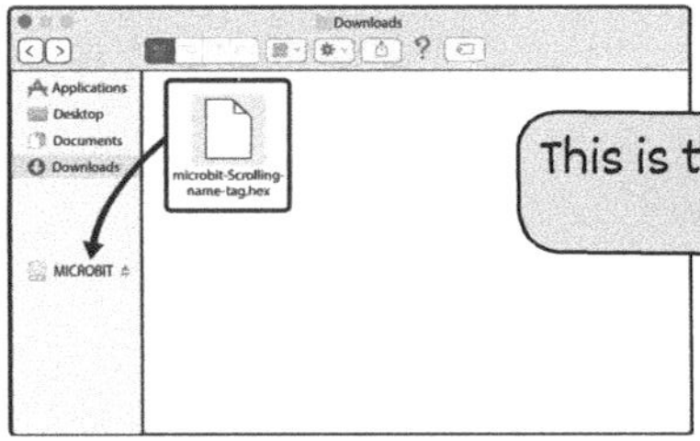

microbit Scrolling
name tag.hex

MICROBIT ⏏

This is the same for both a Mac and PC

Project 2
Animated Display

Our next project will use the micro:bit to make animated LED "GIFs". These will look like chopping scissors and an exploding firework. We are also going to explore inputs using the onboard buttons. We will also learn how to use a few basic programming concepts like **variables** and **if/else conditional statements**. There will also be some suggestions for how to design your own animations.

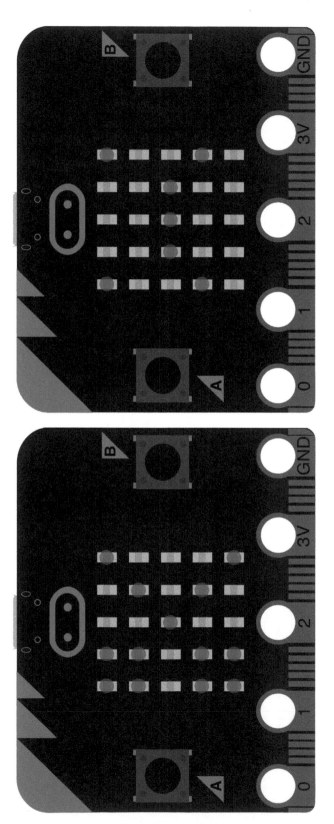

Coding our animations

1 We are going to work with two new code blocks: show icon and show leds. Together these two will help us set which LEDs to turn on first to make our scissors chop and later to create the firework animation. Drag both of these code blocks from the basic section to the coding area.

2 In the show icon block, we are going to click on the blue triangle to open the full menu. We are going to start with the **scissors**, located in the lower right hand corner.

scissor icon

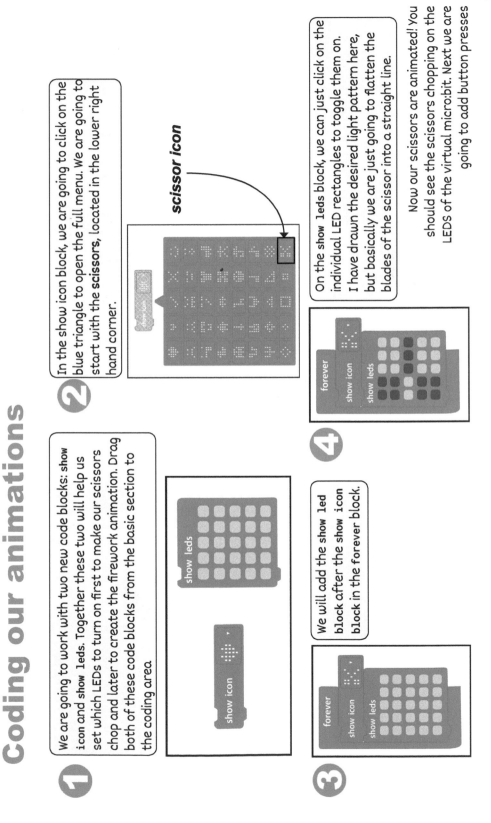

3 We will add the show led block after the show icon block in the forever block.

4 On the show leds block, we can just click on the individual LED rectangles to toggle them on. I have drawn the desired light pattern here, but basically we are just going to flatten the blades of the scissor into a straight line.

Now our scissors are animated! You should see the scissors chopping on the LEDs of the virtual micro:bit. Next we are going to add button presses

5 We need to go into the Input block and select the on button code block and drag it into the code area

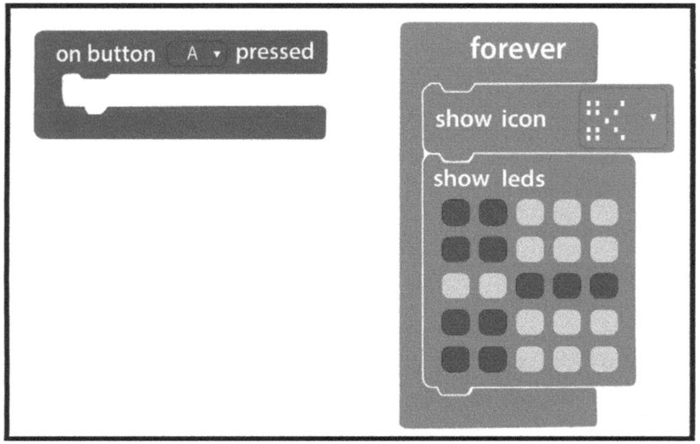

6 Attach the show icon and show leds to the on button A pressed. We can then click on forever and hit the delete key. Grab a second on button code block, hit the triangle drop down, and select the B button.

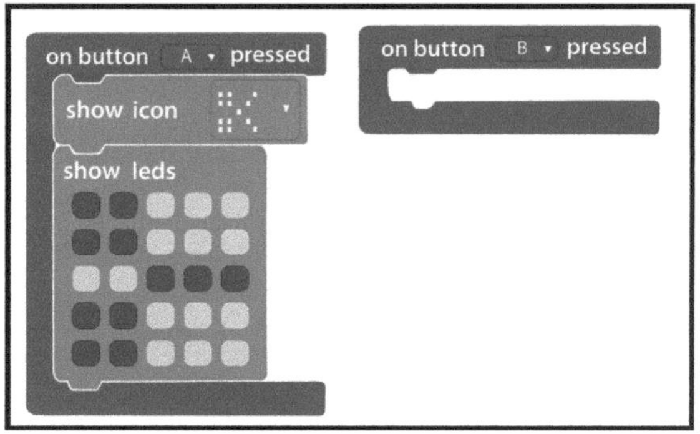

7 Under the on button B, we can copy and paste multiple show leds. Each of these blocks acts like a single frame of animation. Shown here is the first 5 frames for our firework animation.

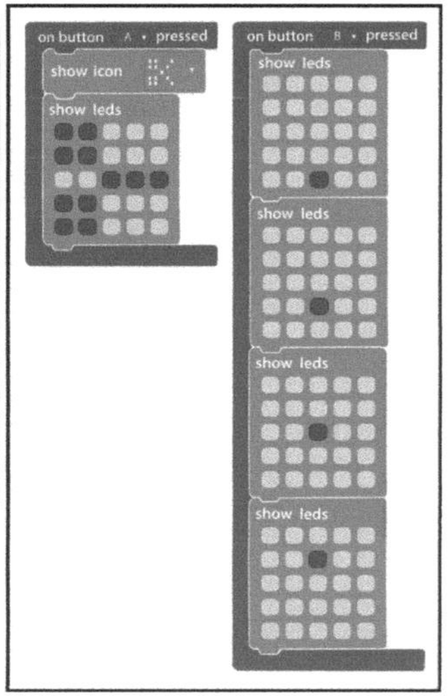

8 It takes nine total frames to make our firework animation, which includes one blank frame with no lights on at the end. All nine blocks are stacked in order and should be contained under the on button B press as in our previous diagram.

Feel free to add as many frames as you want to this or any animation!

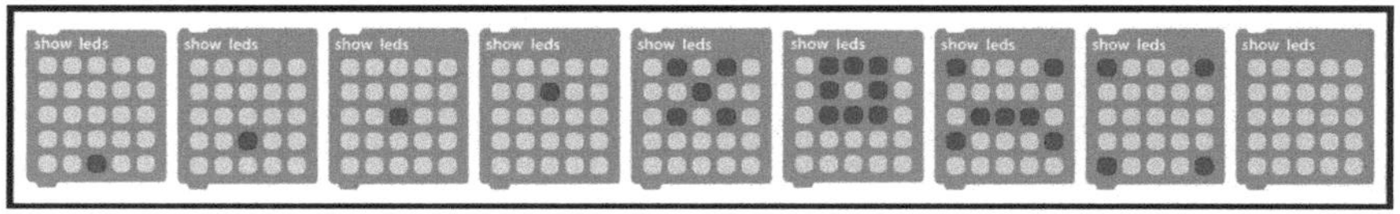

We are going to add one more step to ensure that each animation plays continuously once the corresponding button is pressed. To accomplish this, we are going to make a **variable**, and use a **conditional IF/THEN** statement. We will also add to make it so that pressing both the A and B button will turn the animations off.

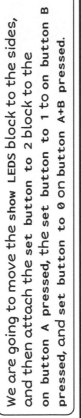

1

First enter the Variable menu, and at the top select **Make a Variable**

At the pop up menu, we are going to name our variable button.

Drag the button variable into the code area.

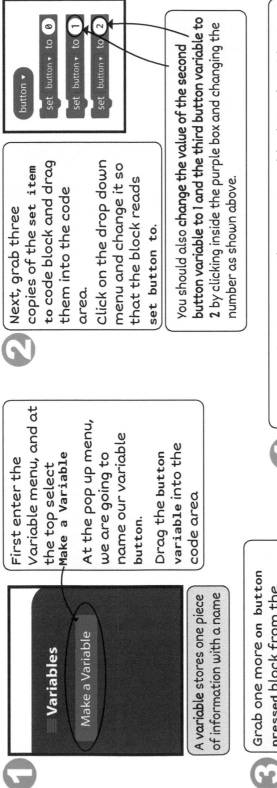

Variables

Make a Variable

A variable stores one piece of information with a name

2

Next, grab three copies of the set item to code block and drag them into the code area.

Click on the drop down menu and change it so that the block reads set button to.

You should also change the value of the second button variable to 1 and the third button variable to 2 by clicking inside the purple box and changing the number as shown above.

3

Grab one more on button pressed block from the input menu. We are also going to add that when we press A and B the animations turn off.

on button A+B ▾ pressed

4

We are going to move the show LEDS block to the sides, and then attach the set button to 2 block to the on button A pressed, the set button to 1 to on button B pressed, and set button to 0 on button A+B pressed.

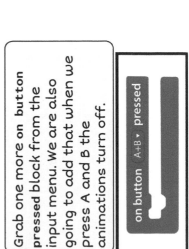

13

5 Next we are going to click on the Logic menu. we will use the "If then else" conditional block, the second from the top.

A **conditional statement** will perform different actions if a condition is met.

6 Click on the white **plus** icon in the lower left corner to add an additonal **else if** to the conditional statement.

7 Drag two conditional blocks to the code area. These blocks will help us figure out which action to take with our conditional.

Comparison

8 Make a copy of the **button** variable, then drag one button variable into the first sectionof the comparison block. Next, change the number to 2. Do the same with the other comparison block, and change the number to 1.

These **comparison statements** let us evaluate if the listed statement is **True.**

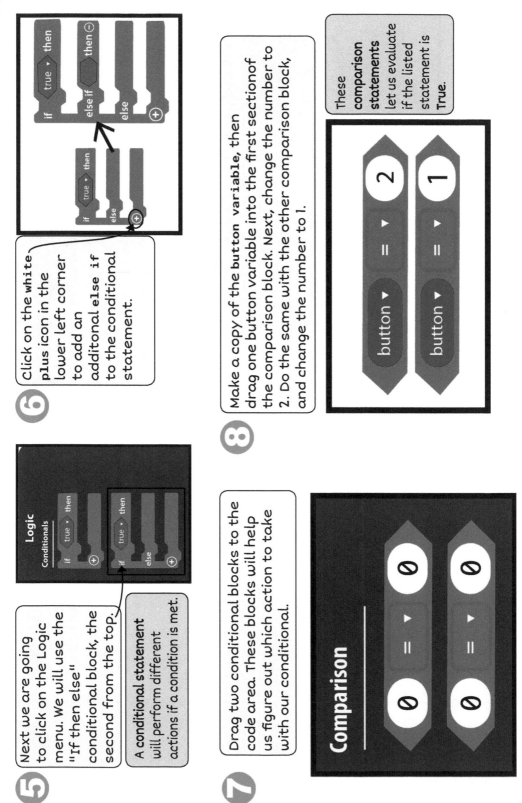

9 Attach the first comparison block variable to the if box, then attach the scissor animation below the if statement.

With conditionals, it helps to say the results out loud in plain language. "If I press the A button, the scissor animation will loop."

10 Finally, attach the the other comparison block to the else if section, and the firework animation to the corresponding then section. This way, if we push the B button our fireworks animation will play!

We will leave the last else blank, since when we push both A and B the button variable is equal to zero, nothing will be displayed, clearing the animations.

Rename the project to Animated Display, upload your code to your microbit and show off your animated gifs!

That's it! Now each of our animations will loop forever, until another button combination is pressed.

When we push button A, we change the value of the button variable to two, and loop the scissor animation.

If we push button 'B,' this changes the button variable value to one, which loops the fireworks animation.

If we push both 'A' and 'B' at the same time, the animations will turn off.

Project 3
Wayfind Plus, a high tech compass

This next project will have us creating an **electronic compass**, with LEDs to point us North and south. This will also have us build our **first electric circuits** off the micro:bit and explore the various types of wiring available for future projects. We will also load our code from the computer and then power our micro:bit from a **AA battery pack** to make it portable.

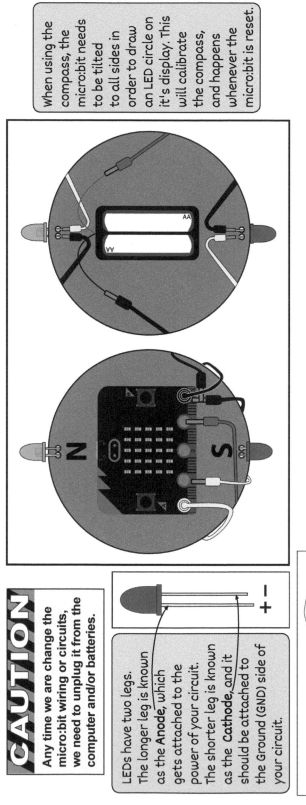

When using the compass, the micro:bit needs to be tilted to all sides in order to draw an LED circle on it's display. This will calibrate the compass, and happens whenever the micro:bit is reset.

We are going to start by looking at the various ways to attach electronic components to our micro:bit. For this project we are going to use both **Banana plugs** and **Alligator clips**.

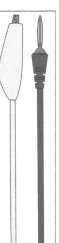

CAUTION

Any time we are change the micro:bit wiring or circuits, we need to unplug it from the computer and/or batteries.

LEDs have two legs. The longer leg is known as the **Anode**, which gets attached to the power of your circuit. The shorter leg is known as the **Cathode**, and it should be attached to the Ground (GND) side of your circuit.

Banana plugs and Alligator clips

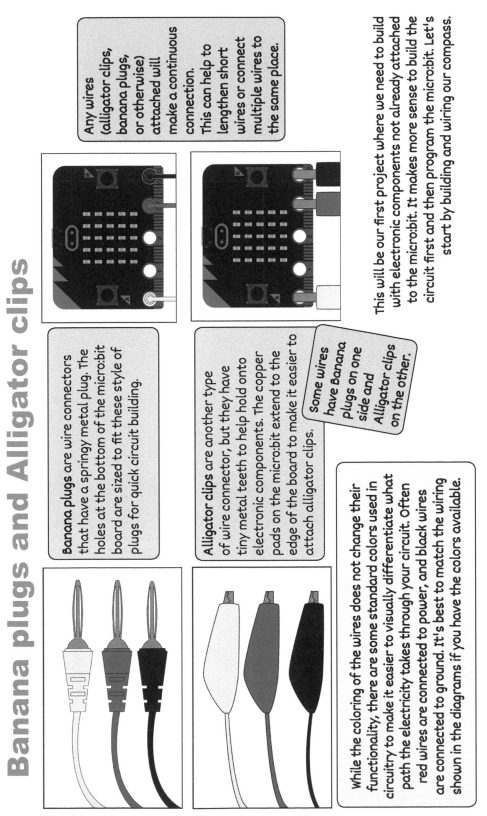

Banana plugs are wire connectors that have a springy metal plug. The holes at the bottom of the micro:bit board are sized to fit these style of plugs for quick circuit building.

Alligator clips are another type of wire connector, but they have tiny metal teeth to help hold onto electronic components. The copper pads on the micro:bit extend to the edge of the board to make it easier to attach alligator clips.

Some wires have Banana plugs on one side and Alligator clips on the other.

Any wires (alligator clips, banana plugs, or otherwise) attached will make a continuous connection.

This can help to lengthen short wires or connect multiple wires to the same place.

While the coloring of the wires does not change their functionality, there are some standard colors used in circuitry to make it easier to visually differentiate what path the electricity takes through your circuit. Often red wires are connected to power, and black wires are connected to ground. It's best to match the wiring shown in the diagrams if you have the colors available.

This will be our first project where we need to build with electronic components not already attached to the micro:bit. It makes more sense to build the circuit first and then program the micro:bit. Let's start by building and wiring our compass.

Building and wiring Wayfind Plus

1 Using scissors, Cut a 5 inch circle out of thin cardboard. Poke two small holes on the top and bottom of the circle about 1/2 an inch apart. Using a marker, write N near one set of holes, and S near the other.

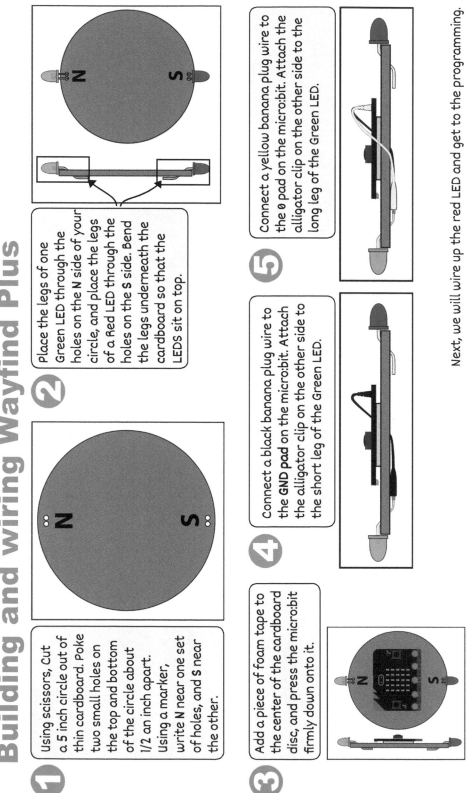

2 Place the legs of one Green LED through the holes on the N side of your circle, and place the legs of a Red LED through the holes on the S side. Bend the legs underneath the cardboard so that the LEDS sit on top.

3 Add a piece of foam tape to the center of the cardboard disc, and press the micro:bit firmly down onto it.

4 Connect a black banana plug wire to the **GND pad** on the micro:bit. Attach the alligator clip on the other side to the short leg of the Green LED.

5 Connect a yellow banana plug wire to the **0 pad** on the micro:bit. Attach the alligator clip on the other side to the long leg of the Green LED.

Next, we will wire up the red LED and get to the programming.

6 Connect a black alligator clip to the **GND** pad on the micro:bit. Attach the alligator clip on the other side to the short leg of the red LED.

You can use foam tape to temporarily hold your wires in place, or you can add a small amount of hot glue between the wire and the cardboard for a longer-term hold.

7 Connect a yellow alligator clip to the 1 pad on the micro:bit. Attach the alligator clip on the other side to the long leg of the red LED.

That's it for wiring. Now we can attach the USB cord and begin programming. We will be using a lot of the same code blocks from our last project, but this time with more complicated comparisons. We are also going to use analog sensor readings, namely the compass heading, which is measured in degrees.

Compass degrees go to 360. They start at 0 for North, 90 for East, 180 for South, 270 for West, and back to North at 360.

In addition to the compass heading, the micro:bit offers up a number of other onboard sensor readings. Take a look in the Input list to see more options.

1 Start a new code project. Go into the variable menu and make a new variable named direction. Grab the set item to 0 block, and change the drop down to direction. Next, go into the Input menu and grab the compass heading. Finally, attach the compass heading to the set direction to and place it connected to the forever block.

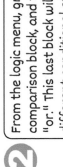

2 From the logic menu, grab the 'if-then' block, the comparison block, and the boolean block that says "or." This last block will allow us to compare two different conditional statements. Also get a copy of your direction variable from the variable menu.

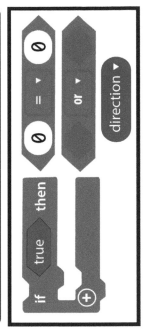

4

Since North can also be 360 degrees, we need to check if it is close in the opposite direction. Let's check if our direction variable is either less than 20 or greater than 340. > or greater than is found in the drop down menu. Duplicate the first comparison, change the comparison to greater than, and the number to 340. Then stick it into the other side of the or block.

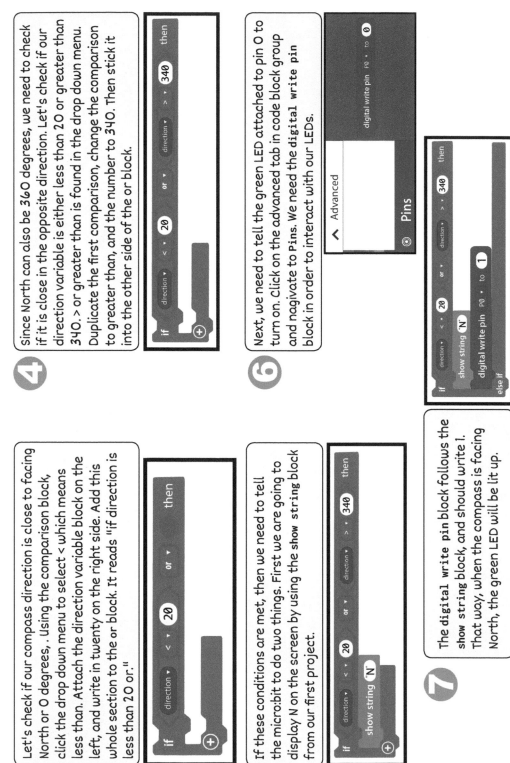

6

Next, we need to tell the green LED attached to pin 0 to turn on. Click on the advanced tab in code block group and navigate to Pins. We need the digital write pin block in order to interact with our LEDs.

3

Let's check if our compass direction is close to facing North or 0 degrees. Using the comparison block, click the drop down menu to select < which means less than. Attach the direction variable block on the left, and write in twenty on the right side. Add this whole section to the or block. It reads "if direction is less than 20 or."

5

If these conditions are met, then we need to tell the micro:bit to do two things. First we are going to display N on the screen by using the show string block from our first project.

7

The digital write pin block follows the show string block, and should write 1. That way, when the compass is facing North, the green LED will be lit up.

We could instead include a show leds that is blank, but this way our code looks similar for each step of the conditional.

8 Click the + sign to add the else if to our conditional block. Then we can copy each block from the North direction of our compass. To check if we are facing south, our direction variable should be less than 200, but greater than 160. Then, we should display **s** and write on, or 1, to our P1 pin.

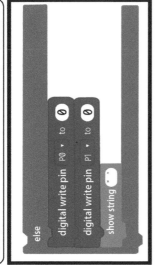

```
else if    direction ▾ < ▾ 200    or ▾    direction ▾ > ▾ 160    then
    show string "S"
    digital write pin P1 ▾ to 1
else
```

9 Finally, we have to add code to our else statement. If we are neither facing North, nor South, we are going to turn off our LEDs, and display a blank string to clear the screen.

```
else
    digital write pin P0 ▾ to 0
    digital write pin P1 ▾ to 0
    show string ""
```

That's all the code our compass requires! Upload the code to your micro:bit. Once the code is done uploading, the micro:bit will automatically begin the calibration process. Tilt your digital compass in order to fill in all the LEDs on the screen.

We just have one last step for our circuit! Now that we have finished uploading the code, we can remove the USB cord and attach our 2AA battery holder.

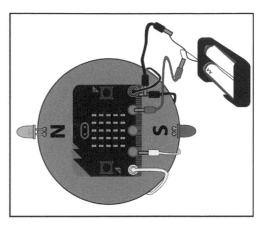

Attach an red alligator wire from the red wire of our 2 AA battery holder to the 3 volt pad on the micro:bit. Attach a black alligator wire from the black wire on the battery holder to the GND port on the micro:bit. Finally, use foam tape to attach the battery holder to the backside of the cardboard. Now that our compass is portable, carry it around your house and try it out!

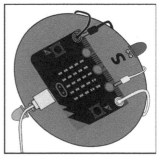

Project 4
Strength Tester

For this project we are going to create a carnival-inspired **Strength Tester**, using the LED grid and a chain of LEDS. We are going to employ an external **Analog Sensor** for this project, using a **Force Sensing Resistor (FSR)** to determine how hard someone is pushing on the strength testing area. We are going to also use a **micro:bit Edge Connector Breakout Board** and a **Breadboard** in order to make this circuit easier to wire.

Each row in the breadboard has electric connectivity. Rows do not connect across the trench that runs down the middle of the board.

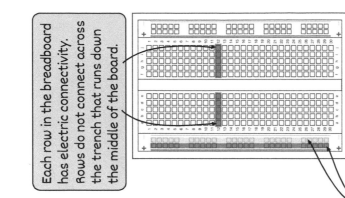

The columns on the edge are called the 'buses' and they are electrically connected. This makes it easier to access the commonly used power and ground pins on the micro:bit.

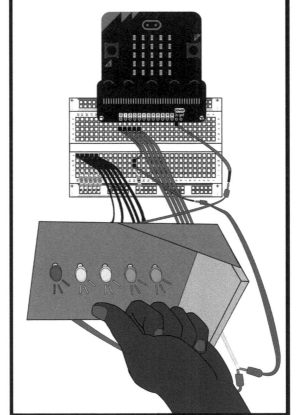

As with our compass project, we will start by building and wiring the our strength tester before programming the micro:bit.

Jumper wires are small electrical wires with special metal tips that make them easier to insert into and remove from breadboards. We will use the jumper wires alongside our alligator clips.

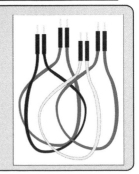

Building the Strength Tester

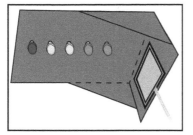

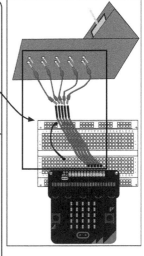

1 Cut out a rectangle with triangle flaps similar to the picture on the right. This will hold our LEDs and the FSR. Score along the dotted lines to make it easier to fold. Poke five pairs of holes into the upper rectangle. It should be close to x inches in length and y inches wide.

Feel free to color your cardboard any way you see fit! It's easier to do while it's still flat.

2 Bend the front rectangle upward to create a 90 degree angle. Bend the triangle flaps inward and secure with clear tape or a small drop of hot glue. Place five LEDs into the holes on the back. Attach the FSR to the base using foam tape.

5 Attach a jumper to the pins labeled **1, 2, 5, 8, and 11**. Then attach alligator clips from these jumper wires to the longer legs of the LEDs in our strength tester. 1 should go to our LED at the bottom, 2 to the second from the bottom, and continue in order to the top.

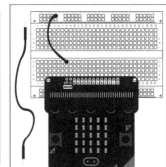

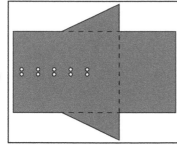

3 Attach your Edge Connector to breadboard, making sure that it is pushed fully into the board. Then insert your micro:bit.

Your edge connector might look different, but should function the same way!

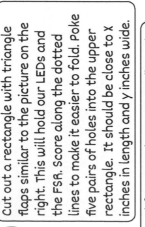

4 Attach a jumper wire from the GND port on the micro:bit to the Ground bus on the breadboard.

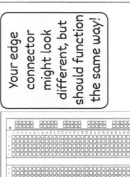

Resistors protect our other components and help to regulate the power in our circuit. We will use two main values of resistors in this book, 220 Ohm and 10k Ohm. We use both in this project.

220 Ohm
(red, red, brown)

10 kOhm
(brown, black, orange)

6 Add five jumper wires to the breadboard. Connect each jumper to an alligator clip, and the alligator clip to the short leg of an LED. Add a 220 Ohm resistor (red, red, brown gold bands) from the other end of the jumper to the ground bus for each LED.

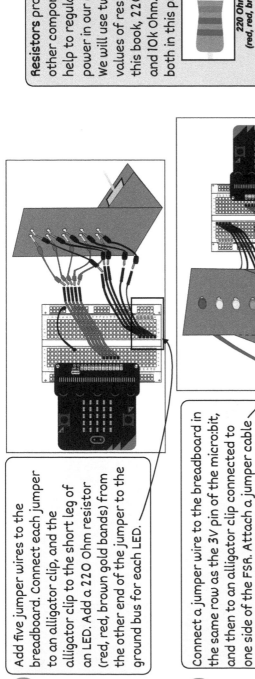

7 Connect a jumper wire to the breadboard in the same row as the 3V pin of the micro:bit, and then to an alligator clip connected to one side of the FSR. Attach a jumper cable to Pin 0, and then to another row on the breadboard. Add a 10kOhm resistor from the jumper to the Ground bus. In between the resistor and the jumper to Pin 0, attach a second jumper to an alligator clip, and the remaining open FSR pin.

8 Cut a piece of foam approximately the size of your strength tester base. Attach this piece of foam lightly on top of the FSR, using foam tape around its edges.

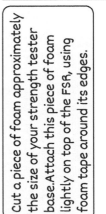

Now that our project is put together, we can begin programming the micro:bit. Most of what we use for this project will look familiar from the compass (conditionals, variables, using pins), but we will also be using an Analog value from the FSR which is our first time taking sensor data from something not part of the micro:bit. Let's take a look.

Programming our Strength Tester

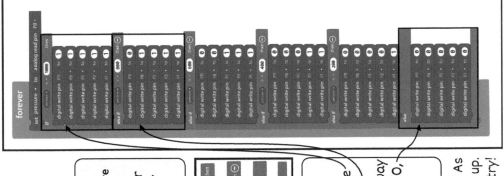

1 Let's start by making a new variable named pressure. Grab the set pressure to code block from the variable menu. Then grab the analog read pin block from the pin menu, which is hidden under the advanced tab.

Digital sensors give a value of either 0 or 1. **Analog sensors** will give a range of values. For this project, our Force Sensing resistor (FSR) will give us a numerical value between 0 and 1023.

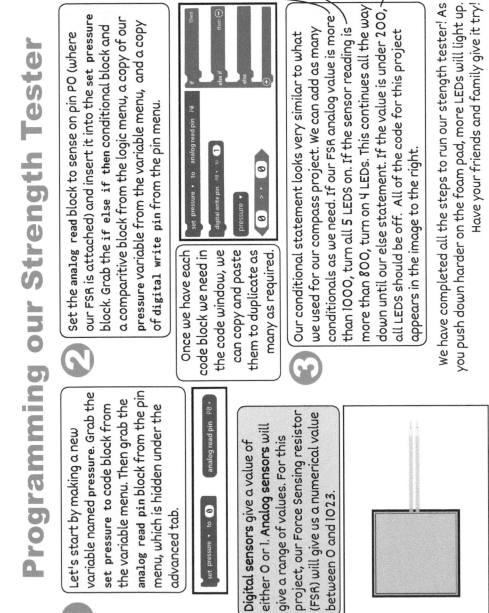

2 Set the analog read block to sense on pin P0 (where our FSR is attached and insert it into the set pressure block. Grab the if then else block from the logic menu, a copy of our pressure variable from the variable menu, and a copy of digital write pin from the pin menu.

Once we have each code block we need in the code window, we can copy and paste them to duplicate as many as required.

3 Our conditional statement looks very similar to what we used for our compass project. We can add as many conditionals as we need. If our FSR analog value is more than 1000, turn all 5 LEDS on. If the sensor reading is more than 800, turn on 4 LEDs. This continues all the way down until our else statement. If the value is under 200, all LEDS should be off. All of the code for this project appears in the image to the right.

We have completed all the steps to run our strength tester! As you push down harder on the foam pad, more LEDs will light up. Have your friends and family give it try!

Project 5
Tilt! A handheld tilting game

It's time to make a game. We are going to create Tilt! It's a game based on moving our character to catch falling objects. In this game, we play a farmer collecting apples. We play the entire game on the LEDs on the front of our micro:bit, controlling the play by just tilting our handheld controller. We will use the onboard **accelerometer** to measure the tilt of our device, and we will add a **speaker** so that we can hear sound effects and the intro music to our game. We will learn a few new programming concepts, including making our own **functions**, and **loading extensions** for additional programmatic capabilities.

Tilt! can be about catching any falling thing that you want, in which case you may change the variable names.

Functions allow us to perform many actions with a single line of code. Rather than copying the same code, we can just trigger or **call** the function whenever we need to perform the set of actions.

This call function block will execute these two commands everytime the program sees the function call block, whether in a loop, a conditional, or nested inside another function.

A sprite is a game term for any character or element included in the game

Let's get started by cutting some cardboard and building our next circuit.

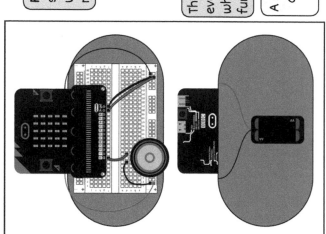

An **accelerometer** measures the change in acceleration. The micro:bit has this hardware sensor already installed. As a reminder it is labeled on the back of the micro:bit. To use the sensor, we just have to access it through code.

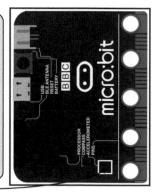

Assembling the Tilt Controller

1

Cut a rounded rectangle out of cardboard. It should be sligthly wider and longer than a breadboard. Attach the breadboard to the cardboard with foam tape. Insert the edge connector into the breadboard and attach the micro:bit.

2

Add a jumper wire from the ground pin of the edge connector to the ground bus, and another from the 3V pin to the power bus. Push the speaker into the breadboard, and attach a jumper from pin 0 to one side of the speaker. Attach the other side of the speaker to the ground bus.

3

Attach the battery pack onto the back of the game controller in the center of the cardboard using a piece of foam tape. We won't attach the batteries to our breadboard until after we have programmed our Tilt! game.

Our game will address our location in the LED grid by using an **Array**. With arrays, computer programs start counting at zero rather than one. The first row of LEDs is row zero. We will use this to move our character and control where the "apples" drop.

Our gamepad for Tilt! is now complete. Attach the USB cable to your micro:bit and we can begin programming our game.

Programming Tilt!

Rather than doing step by step instructions as we have for our previous coding, it makes more sense for this project to look at the separate steps involved in our game. This will also help to tackle functions as we can look at each function individually. In order to make this programming as streamlined as possible, we are going to start by adding an extension.

In a number of other programing languages, extensions are known as libraries.

We have four basic concepts in our game that we have to control. We will give each one of these concepts a function. This will also be our first time using on start in addition to the forever block.

We are going to cover the forever block first, but let's line up the four concepts for our functions. These are:

1. **Move our player character**

2. **Create "apples" (lit Red LEDs) at the top of the LED grid**

3. **Move the "apples"**

4. **Check to see if the "apples" touch our character**

If you can't find the block you are looking for, you can always use the search function at the top of the code block groups.

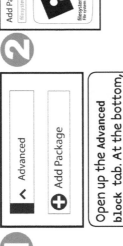

Open up the Advanced block tab. At the bottom, select Add Package.

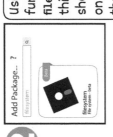

Using the search function, enter filesystem. When this extension shows up, click on it to return to the code window

Here we have our forever function. To make these new function blocks, we can enter the Function tab under the Advanced section and select create function. We also use blocks from the Math, Input, Control, Logic, Basic, and Variable sections.

If the absolute value of the acceleration is greater than 100, we will move our character.

call the moveCharacter function

If it has been longer than 500 milliseconds (running time minus our time variable), drop the "apple".

call the moveApples function

If A+B buttons are pressed together, then reset the program

reset, which will restart the program

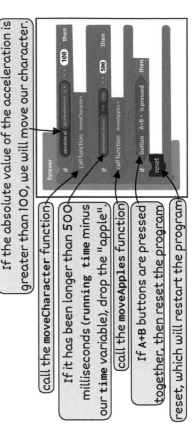

1 Moving our player character

In this function, we will scale the acceleration value (how tilted our micro:bit is) to the position of our character on the screen. Our character will equal a number between 0 and 4, to set our position on the screen

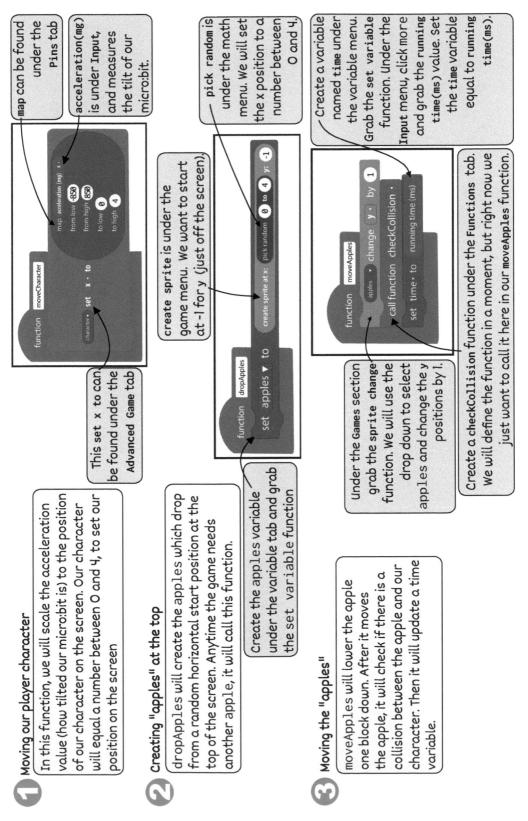

map can be found under the Pins tab

acceleration(mg) is under Input, and measures the tilt of our micro:bit.

This set x to can be found under the Advanced Game tab

2 Creating "apples" at the top

dropApples will create the apples which drop from a random horizontal start position at the top of the screen. Anytime the game needs another apple, it will call this function.

Create the apples variable under the variable tab and grab the set variable function

create sprite is under the game menu. We want to start at -1 for y (just off the screen).

pick random is under the math menu. We will set the x position to a number between 0 and 4.

3 Moving the "apples"

moveApples will lower the apple one block down. After it moves the apple, it will check if there is a collision between the apple and our character. Then it will update a time variable.

Under the Games section grab the sprite change function. We will use the drop down to select apples and change the y positions by 1.

Create a checkCollision function under the Functions tab. We will define the function in a moment, but right now we just want to call it here in our moveApples function.

Create a variable named time under the variable menu. Grab the set variable function. Under the Input menu, click more and grab the running time(ms) value. Set the time variable equal to running time(ms).

Finally we will add to our on start block. We need to load the saved high score from the file system back into our program, create our player character, and create the first "apple" to drop.

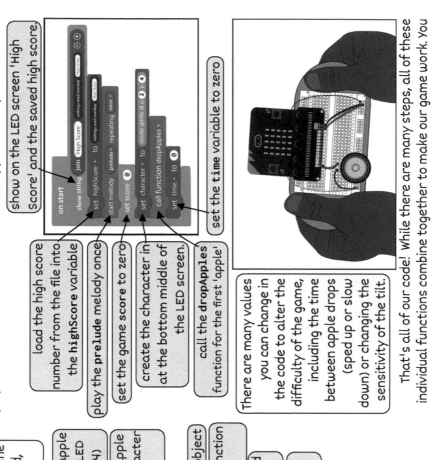

show on the LED screen 'High Score' and the saved high score.

load the high score number from the file into the highScore variable

play the prelude melody once

set the game score to zero

create the character in at the bottom middle of the LED screen.

call the dropApples function for the first 'apple'

set the time variable to zero

There are many values you can change in the code to alter the difficulty of the game, including the time between apple drops (sped up or slow down) or changing the sensitivity of the tilt.

That's all of our code! While there are many steps, all of these individual functions combine together to make our game work. You are ready to play Tilt!

4 check to see if the "apples" touch our character

checkCollision evaluates whether the falling apple touches our player character. If it does, we increase the score and play a noise. If the apple falls to the ground, we trigger a series of game over events.

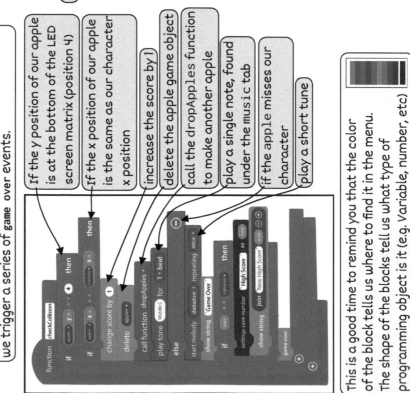

If the y position of our apple is at the bottom of the LED screen matrix (position 4)

If the x position of our apple is the same as our character x position

increase the score by 1

delete the apple game object

call the dropApples function to make another apple

play a single note, found under the music tab

if the apple misses our character

play a short tune

This is a good time to remind you that the color of the block tells us where to find it in the menu. The shape of the blocks tell us what type of programming object is it (e.g. Variable, number, etc)

Project 6
Cooling hat

With all of this hard work our head must be getting quite warm. To fix this we are going to create a cooling hat, one that has a fan on either side, starting our foray into creating projects that move. Again, we will rely on the battery pack to make our hat portable, but this time we will use a **4AA battery pack**, which supplies more power. We will also use a **Voltage Regulator** to control the voltage, and a **motor driver** to trigger the fans. We will also attach a **tri-color LED** as a visual indicator for the temperature. Once we have built the project, we can experiment with a variety of ways to trigger the hat, from simple button pushes to gestures like head tilting.

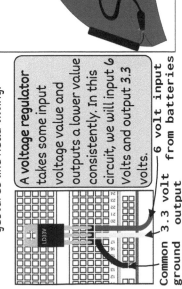

A **voltage regulator** takes some input voltage value and outputs a lower value consistently. In this circuit, we will input 6 Volts and output 3.3 volts.

Common 3.3 volt output 6 volt input
ground from batteries

We are using **5 volt fans.** Each fan should have a power wire and a ground wire, usually red and black. This sort of fan also has easily accessible mounting holes.

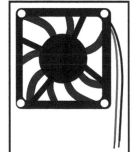

There is a bit more fabrication for this project than before, including a little bit of sewing to keep the fans in place. We are going to fabricate our hat, build our circuit, and then put them together. Once we built the project, we will get into writing our code.

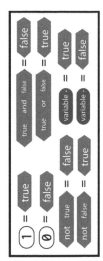

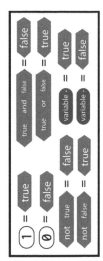

While we have used the concept in earlier projects, our cooling hat relies heavily on **boolean logic**. Boolean logic refers to the truth of a statement.

1 = true
0 = false

true and false = false
true or false = true

not true = false
not false = true

variable = true
variable = false

We will look at whether the value of our boolean variable is either 1 (true) or 0 (false). We will also use the logic operator not. Not changes false to true, or true to false. We will also set new variables directly to boolean.

CAUTION

Be careful with the fan! We will put some mesh to prevent catching your hair in the fan when wearing the hat, but make sure not to put any fingers or electronics near the fan blades.

Building our hat and circuit

1 Using the scissors, start by cutting a hole on either side of the hat slightly smaller than the fan. Pierce the front middle of the hat bill, and use the tip of the scissors to widen the hole to fit an LED through.

2 Place one fan on top of one of the holes. Using the sewing needle, loop thread through one of the screw holes on the corner of the fan into the hat. Repeat several times until the fan is firmly attached to the hat and repeat for all four holes and again for the second fan. Attach a small piece of mesh on the inside of the hat over the fan using a few drops of hot glue. Run the wires from the fans across the brim of the hat, and use the hot glue gun to add a dot of hot glue to hold the wires in place.

Make sure to sew several loops around each fan mounting hole to keep the fans secured to the hat.

3 Stick the tri-color LED through the hole in the brim with the bulb-side down. Use a dot of hot glue to secure it in place, and bend the four legs apart so they are not touching

4 Place the edge connector into the top of the breadboard, and slide the micro:bit into the edge connector. Attach the ground of the micro:bit to the ground bus using a jumper. Attach both ground buses together using a jumper.

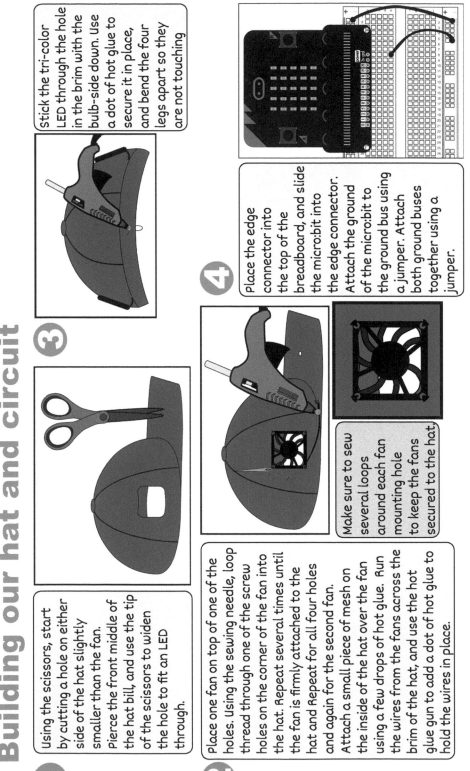

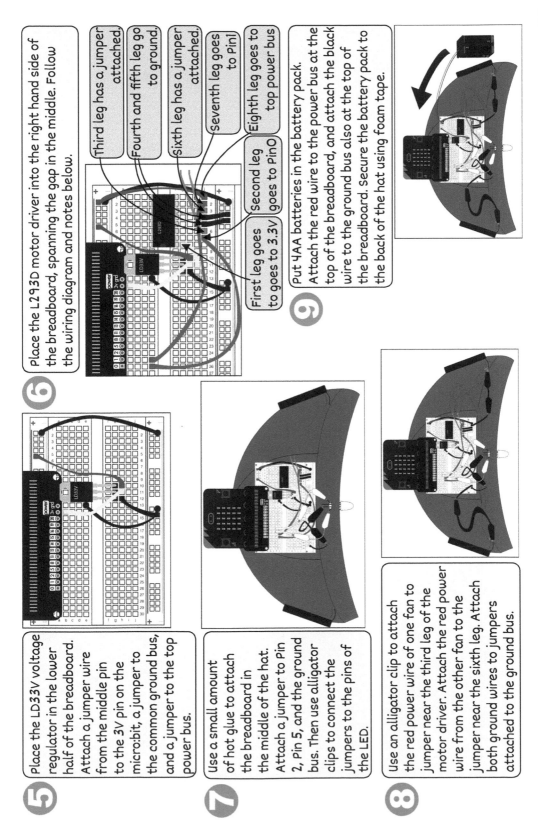

5 Place the LD33V voltage regulator in the lower half of the breadboard. Attach a jumper wire from the middle pin to the 3V pin on the micro:bit, a jumper to the common ground bus, and a jumper to the top power bus.

6 Place the L293D motor driver into the right hand side of the breadboard, spanning the gap in the middle. Follow the wiring diagram and notes below.

Third leg has a jumper attached.

Fourth and fifth leg go to ground.

Sixth leg has a jumper attached.

Seventh leg goes to Pin1

Eighth leg goes to top power bus

Second leg goes to Pin0

First leg goes to goes to 3.3V

7 Use a small amount of hot glue to attach the breadboard in the middle of the hat. Attach a jumper to Pin 2, Pin 5, and the ground bus. Then use alligator clips to connect the jumpers to the pins of the LED.

8 Use an alligator clip to attach the red power wire of one fan to jumper near the third leg of the motor driver. Attach the red power wire from the other fan to the jumper near the sixth leg. Attach both ground wires to jumpers attached to the ground bus.

9 Put 4AA batteries in the battery pack. Attach the red wire to the power bus at the top of the breadboard, and attach the black wire to the ground bus also at the top of the breadboard. Secure the battery pack to the back of the hat using foam tape.

33

Coding for the Cooling hat

As with our last project, we are going to explain the individual parts of the code without walking step by step on where to find them in the menu.

Set both boolean fan variables to false

If button A is pressed, set the FanA boolean variable to its opposite. That is, if it is false, make it true and if it is true make it false. Button B does the same for the FanB boolean variable.

This whole function looks at which of FanA and FanB are true, and then displays a string on the LED screen to show which fans should be active.

That's all we need. Keep in mind that you could always trigger the fans by looking at other values, like the temperature, compass direction, or lighting levels.

If the FanA boolean variable is true, turn on FanA and one color pin of the LED.

If the FanA boolean variable is false, turn off FanA and one color pin of the LED.

If the FanB boolean variable is true, turn on FanB and a different color pin of the LED.

If the FanB boolean variable is false, turn off FanA and one color pin of the LED.

Call the displayFan function to show on the LED screen which fans are activated

If the micro:bit is tilted, turn on both fans and both pins of the LED. Otherwise, turn everyting off

Project 7
Wave-o-tron, a musical instrument

We are now going to build the wave-o-tron, an electronic instrument designed to change both the pitch and the speed of electronic music notes. We will change the **note** by looking at the sensor value of one **photoresistor**, and change the **speed of the note** with a second photoresistor. We will also again play our notes through a speaker, but this time we will discuss **pulse width modulation** which makes this instrument possible.

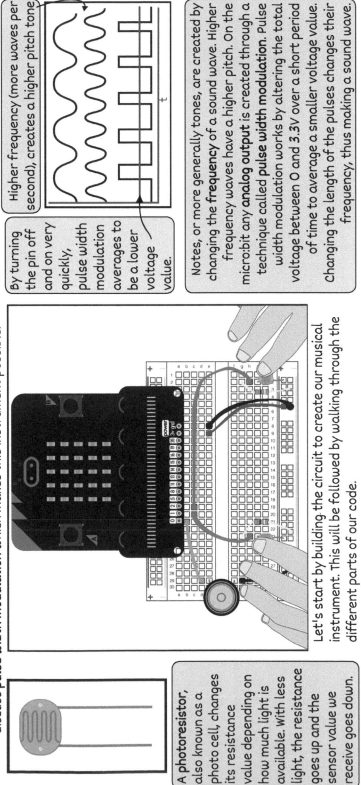

Higher frequency (more waves per second), creates a higher pitch tone

By turning the pin off and on very quickly, pulse width modulation averages to be a lower voltage value.

Notes, or more generally tones, are created by changing the **frequency** of a sound wave. Higher frequency waves have a higher pitch. On the micro:bit any **analog output** is created through a technique called **pulse width modulation**. Pulse width modulation works by altering the total voltage between 0 and 3.3V over a short period of time to average a smaller voltage value. Changing the length of the pulses changes their frequency, thus making a sound wave.

Let's start by building the circuit to create our musical instrument. This will be followed by walking through the different parts of our code.

A photoresistor, also known as a photo cell, changes its resistance value depending on how much light is available. With less light, the resistance goes up and the sensor value we receive goes down.

Constructing the Wave-o-tron

1 Place the edge connector into the top of the breadboard, and slide the micro:bit into the edge connector. Attach the power and the ground of the micro:bit to the power and ground bus using jumpers.

2 Attach one leg of a photo resistor to the power bus on the left side of the breadboard. In the next hole in the same row, attach a jumper wire to Pin 1. Next attach a 10kOhm resistor from the end of the same row to the ground bus.

3 This time, start on the right side of the breadboard. Attach the photo resistor to the power bus, attach a jumper from next to leg of the photo resistor to Pin 2, and attach a 10kOhm resistor from the other side of the jumper to the ground bus.

4 Connect a jumper wire to Pin0. Place the speaker into the breadboard spanning two rows and attach the jumper wire from Pin0 to one side of the speaker. Attach the other side of the speaker to ground.

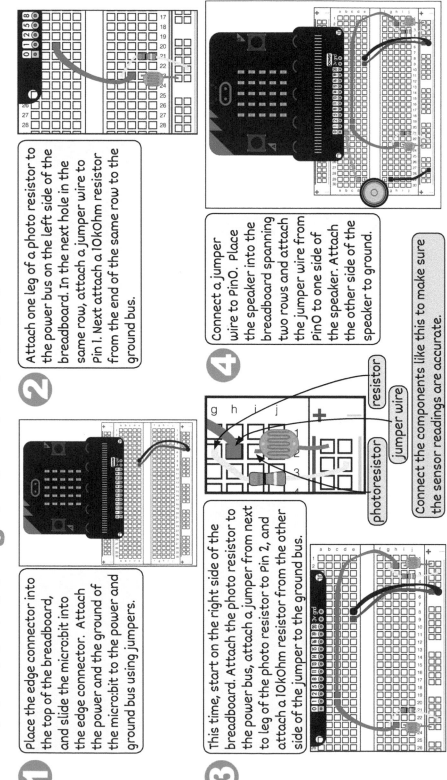

resistor

jumper wire

photoresistor

Connect the components like this to make sure the sensor readings are accurate.

Coding the Wave-o-tron

While our code looks slightly simpler than some of our recent projects, there are a lot of steps packed into this single line. Rather than using variables to store the photo resistor sensor values, we can input the values directly into the play tone function and vary both the pitch and timing.

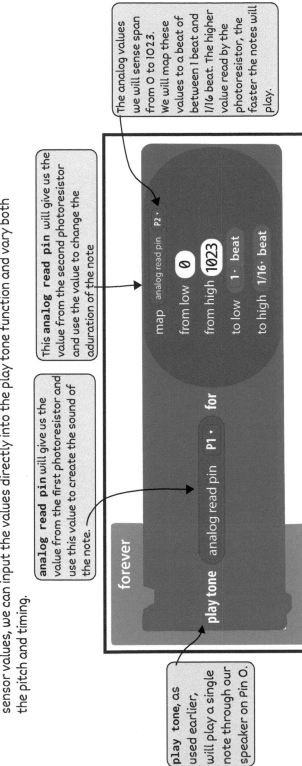

play tone, as used earlier, will play a single note through our speaker on Pin O.

analog read pin will give us the value from the first photoresistor and use this value to create the sound of the note.

This analog read pin will give us the value from the second photoresistor and use the value to change the aduration of the note

The analog values we will sense span from O to IO23. We will map these values to a beat of between I beat and I/I6 beat. The higher value read by the photoresistor, the faster the notes will play.

That's all the code we need for our Wave-o-tron! While the photoresistors work fine in with regular room lighting, the effect is even greater if you use a flashlight. This is one reason we placed the photo resistors on either end of the breadboard. Enjoy learning to play your new Wave-o-tron!

Project 8
Security System

For our next project let's build our own security system. We will use an **infrared LED emitter** which will create an infrared beam. We will also use an **IR collector** to sense when the beam is broken by a person or object. When the beam is broken, we are going to send a message to our computer using **serial communication**. We will load a prewritten **Processing** sketch to receive our serial message and change the color of a program running on our computer.

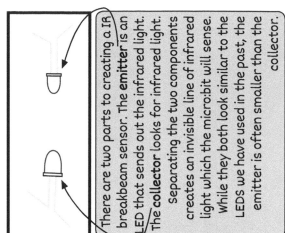

There are two parts to creating a IR breakbeam sensor. The **emitter** is an LED that sends out the infrared light. The **collector** looks for infrared light. Separating the two components creates an invisible line of infrared light which the micro:bit will sense. While they both look similar to the LEDs we have used in the past, the emitter is often smaller than the collector.

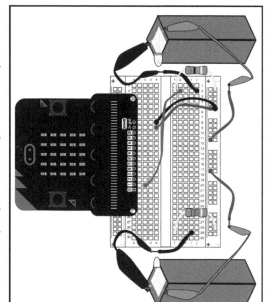

serial communication is protocol that allows us to send messages back and forth between our micro:bit and our computer. In order for this to work, both devices have to be listening to the same place, and speaking at the same pace. The place to listen is called the port, and the speaking pace is called the baud rate. Both of these values will be set automatically by the micro:bit, and we must match them with our **Processing** program.

we will build our circuit, talk about good placement for the IR collector and emitter, and then program the micro:bit. The last step we have to include is loading a program onto our computer to accept the serial communication, and to change a program window a different color each time the beam is broken.

Build our Security system

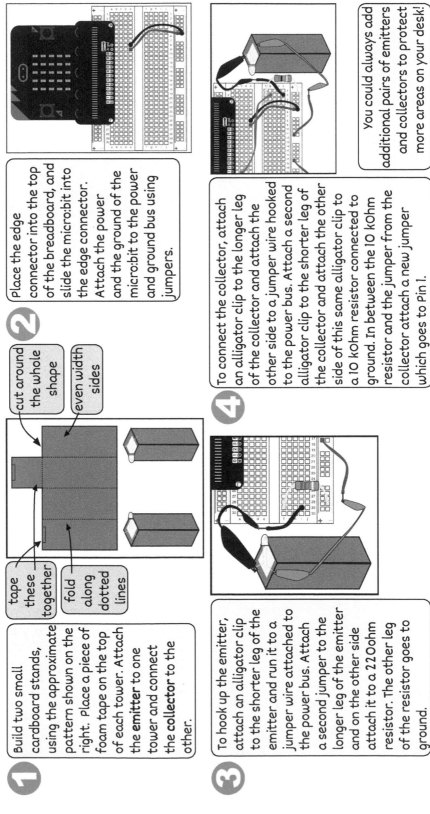

1 Build two small cardboard stands, using the approximate pattern shown on the right. Place a piece of foam tape on the top of each tower. Attach the **emitter** to one tower and connect the **collector** to the other.

cut around the whole shape

tape these together

even width sides

fold along dotted lines

2 Place the edge connector into the top of the breadboard, and slide the micro:bit into the edge connector. Attach the power and the ground of the micro:bit to the power and ground bus using jumpers.

3 To hook up the emitter, attach an alligator clip to the shorter leg of the emitter and run it to a jumper wire attached to the power bus. Attach a second jumper to the longer leg of the emitter and on the other side attach it to a 220ohm resistor. The other leg of the resistor goes to ground.

4 To connect the collector, attach an alligator clip to the longer leg of the collector and attach the other side to a jumper wire hooked to the power bus. Attach a second alligator clip to the shorter leg of the collector and attach the other side of this same alligator clip to a 10 kOhm resistor connected to ground. In between the 10 kOhm resistor and the jumper from the collector attach a new jumper which goes to Pin 1.

You could always add additional pairs of emitters and collectors to protect more areas on your desk!

Coding the Security system

If the sensor readings aren't cooperating, it may be worth checking the alignment of the towers. It can be hard to tell since the light is invisible, but small degrees of rotation can make a large difference.

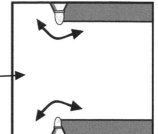

These two functions act as feedback to tell us what our circuit is doing. They will also slow down the responsiveness of our system. If everything is running smoothly, we can delete both of them and reupload our code.

Upload the code to your micro:bit. Next we should tape or otherwise secure the cardboard towers to ensure that the alignment between the emitter and collector gives us a base reading more than the threshhold. We may have to alter the threshold value to change in sensitivity by altering this number. Each time we change the number we will have to upload our code again.

Now that we have written our micro:bit code, we have to download another program named Processing. This will let us use the serial communication to change the color of a program window on our computer.

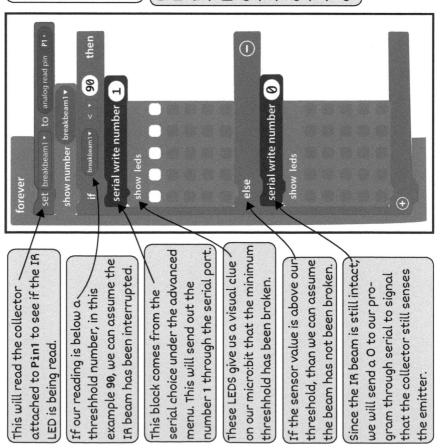

This will read the collector attached to Pin1 to see if the IR LED is being read.

If our reading is below a threshhold number, in this example 90, we can assume the IR beam has been interrupted.

This block comes from the serial choice under the advanced menu. This will send out the number 1 through the serial port.

These LEDS give us a visual clue on our micro:bit that the minimum threshhold has been broken.

If the sensor value is above our threshold, than we can assume the beam has not been broken.

Since the IR beam is still intact, we will send a 0 to our program through serial to signal that the collector still senses the emitter.

Attach to Processing code

1 Go to processing.org. Find your operating system and download the latest version of Processing available. Once it has finished downloading, double click to open the zipped file. Next double click to open the program.

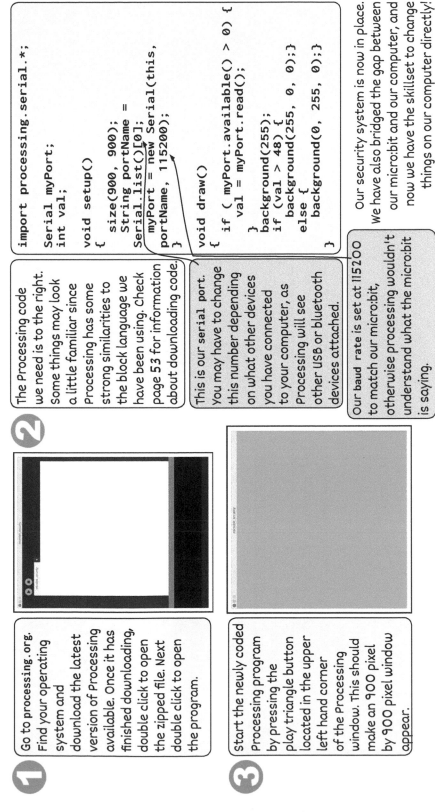

2 The Processing code we need is to the right. Some things may look a little familiar since Processing has some strong similarities to the block language we have been using. Check page 53 for information about downloading code.

This is our serial port. You may have to change this number depending on what other devices you have connected to your computer, as Processing will see other USB or bluetooth devices attached.

Our baud rate is set at 115200 to match our micro:bit, otherwise processing wouldn't understand what the micro:bit is saying.

```
import processing.serial.*;

Serial myPort;
int val;

void setup()
{
    size(900, 900);
    String portName =
Serial.list()[0];
    myPort = new Serial(this,
portName, 115200);
}

void draw()
{
    if ( myPort.available() > 0) {
        val = myPort.read();
    }
    background(255);
    if (val > 48) {
        background(255, 0, 0);}
    else {
        background(0, 255, 0);}
}
```

Our security system is now in place. We have also bridged the gap between our micro:bit and our computer, and now we have the skillset to change things on our computer directly!

3 Start the newly coded Processing program by pressing the play triangle button located in the upper left hand corner of the Processing window. This should make an 900 pixel by 900 pixel window appear.

Project 9
Rolling Robot

Now that we have experimented with a variety of sensors and electronics components, its time to build a robot! Rather than building our robot from scratch, it makes sense to start with a four-wheeled kit; that way we can focus on the wiring and programming instead of building. We will bring back the **motor driver**, but this time we will use it to control **four bi-directional DC motors** attached to wheels. We will use an **ultrasonic rangefinder** and a **passive infrared sensor** to check that the coast is clear in front of our robot, and program it to reverse and turn if the way is not clear.

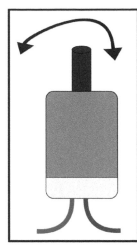

Our robot works with **DC motors** that can spin in both directions. We will use this to make the robot go forward and backward by controlling the direction of the current passing through the motor. The motor driver will make this current control easier, but it does involve a lot of wiring.

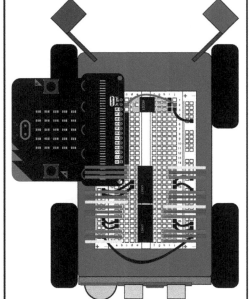

we need to start by assembling the four wheeled robotic kit, which will place all four wheels and motors onto a convenient chassis. We will walk through wiring the robot, before covering programming and different driving behaviors the robot can use.

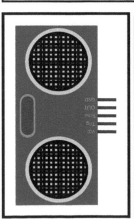

This is an ultrasonic range finder. This sensor works by sending a pulsed ultrasonic wave and measuring how long it takes to bounce off an object and return. We will handle this technique in code by using a new extension. It will be useful for checking if objects are in front of our robot. For more advanced robots, we could include multiple sensors to check all sides.

Assembling the Robot

1 Start by assembling the four-wheeled robot chassis with the included instructions. Make sure that all four motors are secured tightly to the chassis.

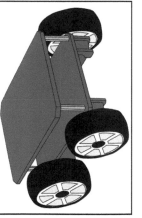

2 Place the edge connector into the top of the breadboard, and slide the micro:bit into the edge connector. Attach the top and bottom ground bus together. Attach the breadboard to the top middle of the robot chassis using foam tape.

3 Attach the LD33CV 3.3 voltatge regulator to the breadboard, and run a jumper from the center pin to the 3.3v on the micro:bit and a jumper from the left pin to the ground bus at the bottom of the breadboard.

4 Next attach two L293D motor drivers next to each other on the left hand side of the breadboard. Add four jumpers to the middle pins of each motor driver that connect to the ground buses.

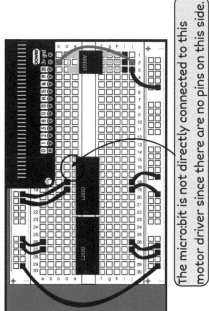

The micro:bit is not directly connected to this motor driver since there are no pins on this side.

5 The wiring diagram to the left lists what each pin of the motor driver gets connected to and is identical for both motor drivers. Each side of the motor driver controls one motor.

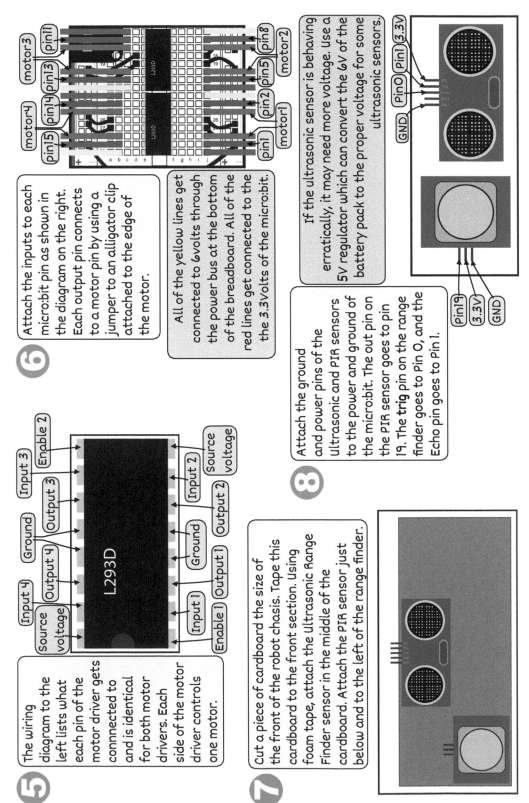

Input 3
Enable 2
Input 4
Output 3
Output 4
Ground
Ground
Output 2
Input 2
L293D
Source voltage
Source voltage
Enable 1
Input 1
Output 1
Output 1

6 Attach the inputs to each micro:bit pin as shown in the diagram on the right. Each output pin connects to a motor pin by using a jumper to an alligator clip attached to the edge of the motor.

All of the yellow lines get connected to 6volts through the power bus at the bottom of the breadboard. All of the red lines get connected to the the 3.3Volts of the micro:bit.

motor3 pin1
motor3
pin13 pin14
motor4
pin15
L293D
L293D
pin1 motor1
pin2 pin5
motor2
pin8 pin2

7 Cut a piece of cardboard the size of the front of the robot chasis. Tape this cardboard to the front section. Using foam tape, attach the Ultrasonic Range Finder sensor in the middle of the cardboard. Attach the PIR sensor just below and to the left of the range finder.

8 Attach the ground and power pins of the ultrasonic and PIR sensors to the power and ground of the micro:bit. The out pin on the PIR sensor goes to pin 19. The **trig** pin on the range finder goes to Pin 0, and the Echo pin goes to Pin 1.

If the ultrasonic sensor is behaving erratically, it may need more voltage. Use a 5V regulator which can convert the 6V of the battery pack to the proper voltage for some ultrasonic sensors.

GND PinO Pin1 3.3V

Pin19
3.3V
GND

With the amount of wires in this project, it can be hard to keep everything neat and clear. For a more complicated project like this one, it makes sense to use twist-ties, zip-ties, or other common cable management systems. You can lock the wires to the body of the robot and know that they won't be able to slide around easily.

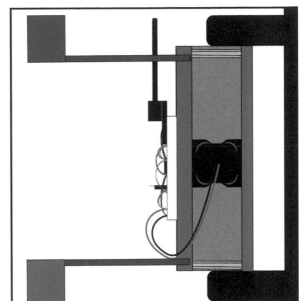

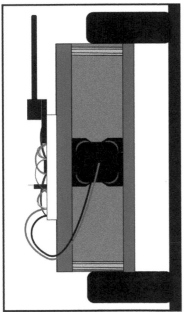

That's it as far as wiring your robot goes. Double check to make sure that all of the wires are securely pressed into and properly aligned within the breadboard. Our next step will be to program some basic techniques and decide how we want our robot to perform.

You are welcome to decorate your robot any way you would like! For my robot, I added red and blue flags to make it easier to identify what direction it is moving from a distance.

9 Finally, load the 4 AA battery holder with four AA batteries. Slide the battery holder into the robot chassis, and attach the ground and power to the buses on the bottom of the breadboard. Run a jumper from the power bus to the right leg of the 3.3V voltage regulator.

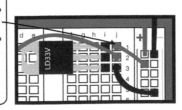

CAUTION

This voltage regulator is where our higher powered battery pack is connected, so we want to be careful when we are adding or removing wires from this area.

Programming our Robot

Just as with our handheld game earlier in the book, it makes sense to break down our robot actions into individual functions which will make creating behaviors a little bit more simple. The general outline of our project is to:

1 Take some sensor readings

2 Evaluate the information

3 Decide what type of drive action our robot should take

Both the sensor readings and the evaluation should take place within our forever code block since this should happen repeatedly as long as our robot is driving around on the ground. Let's look at both of our sensor functions before moving on to our forever block and the driving directions.

When uploading code, it is a good idea to lift your robot off of the table. This is just in case our program tries to power up the motors right away and roll the robot over the edge!

We will set a distance variable equal to the results of running a sonar function. The sonar function evaluates the distance from the sensor to an object by pulsing the trigger pin of the ultrasonic range finder and waiting for the results to come in on the echo pin.

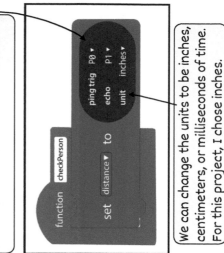

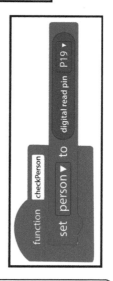

We can change the units to be inches, centimeters, or milliseconds of time. For this project, I chose inches.

Sonar

We need to add the 'Sonar' extension to our code. While it may be possible to create something similar using the basic blocks, Sonar gives us a short cut towards programming the micro:bit to read and understand ultrasonic senors.

The PIR sensor waits for any sort of infrared generating source to appear. This sensor works best with detecting living creatues, either humans or pets. When the sensor detects an event, the light turns on and it sends a singular high command to alert those nearby. We will use pin 19 to take a digital reading, and save this as the person variable.

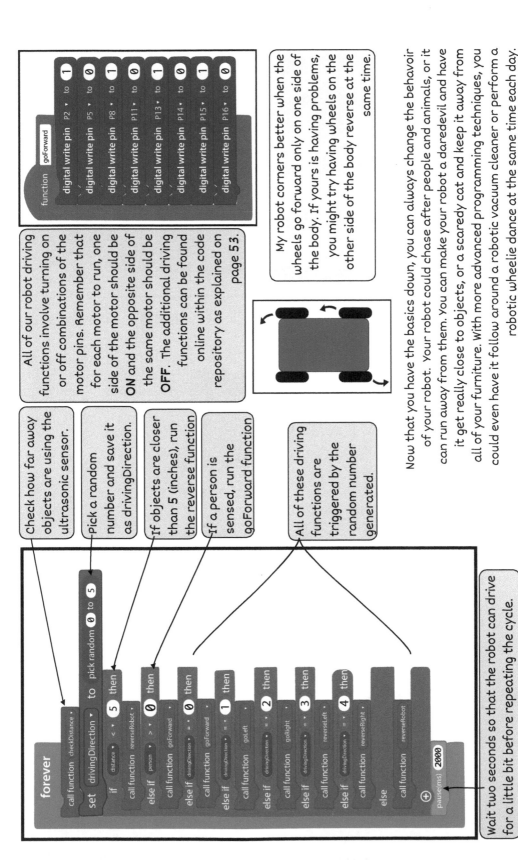

function goForward
- digital write pin P2 ▾ to 1
- digital write pin P5 ▾ to 0
- digital write pin P8 ▾ to 1
- digital write pin P11 ▾ to 0
- digital write pin P13 ▾ to 1
- digital write pin P14 ▾ to 0
- digital write pin P15 ▾ to 1
- digital write pin P16 ▾ to 0

All of our robot driving functions involve turning on or off combinations of the motor pins. Remember that for each motor to run, one side of the motor should be ON and the opposite side of the same motor should be OFF. The additional driving functions can be found online within the code repository as explained on page 53.

My robot corners better when the wheels go forward only on one side of the body. If yours is having problems, you might try having wheels on the other side of the body reverse at the same time.

Check how far away objects are using the ultrasonic sensor.

Pick a random number and save it as drivingDirection.

If objects are closer than 5 (inches), run the reverse function

If a person is sensed, run the goForward function

All of these driving functions are triggered by the random number generated.

```
forever
    call function checkDistance
    set drivingDirection ▾ to pick random 0 to 5
    if distance ▾ < 5 then
        call function reverseRobot
    else if person ▾ > 0 then
        call function goForward
    else if drivingDirection ▾ = 0 then
        call function goForward
    else if drivingDirection ▾ = 1 then
        call function goLeft
    else if drivingDirection ▾ = 2 then
        call function goRight
    else if drivingDirection ▾ = 3 then
        call function reverseLeft
    else if drivingDirection ▾ = 4 then
        call function reverseRight
    else
        call function reverseRobot
    pause(ms) 2000
```

Wait two seconds so that the robot can drive for a little bit before repeating the cycle.

Now that you have the basics down, you can always change the behavior of your robot. Your robot could chase after people and animals, or it can run away from them. You can make your robot a daredevil and have it get really close to objects, or a scaredy cat and keep it away from all of your furniture. With more advanced programming techniques, you could even have it follow around a robotic vacuum cleaner or perform a robotic wheelie dance at the same time each day.

Project 10
Thirsty plant alarm

With all of the work we have done, perhaps we forgot to water our plants! Using a **plant conductivity sensor**, we can check the **resistance** of the soil. If the soil isn't conductive enough, that means that the water content is too low and we should water our plants. We will also attach a **potentiometer** to change how often we take a sensor reading. We will build our project and write our program using the micro:bit blocks, but will also write the code a second time using **Micro:Python**, a second programming language available for micro:bit projects.

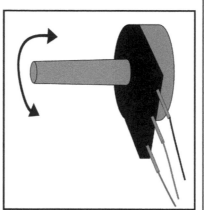

The **potentiometer** is an electronic component that acts as a voltage divider or a changeable resistor, like a volume control knob. Here, we'll use it to set the value at which the plant alarm is triggered.

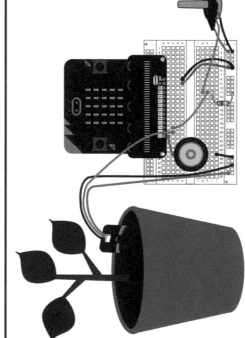

Grab a potted plant nearby and get ready to build your Thirsty plant alarm system. After we create the circuit, we will first complete the code in the micro:bit blocks before introducing MicroPython.

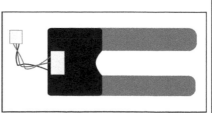

The **soil conductivity sensor** sends out a small electrical current from one leg and measures the results on the other. Soil which is more saturated with water will have higher conductivity.

Building our Thirsty plant alarm

1 Place the edge connector into the top of the breadboard, and slide the micro:bit into the edge connector. Connect the micro:bit to the ground and power buses at the bottom of the breadboard.

2 Place the soil conductivity sensor into your potted plant. The prongs should be fully submerged into the soil. Attach the power and ground wires from the sensor to the power and ground bus. Run the non-red and non-black sensor wire to Pin 1.

3 Attach three alligator clips to the three legs of the potentiometer. One side of the potentiometer gets connected to the ground bus, and the opposite side gets attached to the power bus. The middle pin of the potentiometer connects to a breadboard row, followed by a jumper to Pin 2 and a 10 kOhm resistor attached to ground.

4 Attach our speaker to the breadboard. Attach one side of the speaker to Pin 0, and the other side to the ground bus.

While this book uses the speaker to create the klaxxon to warn us about our plant, you already have the skills to change the project! We could instead have used the tricolor LED, created a change on our computer screen, or activated a motor to wave a flag at us.

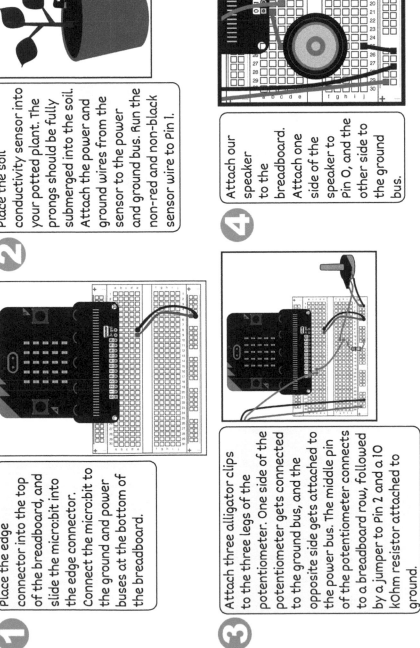

Programming our Thirsty plant alarm

Triggering the sound alarm based on a user controlled device like a potentiometer gives our project two advantages. First, it is easy enough to adjust this threshold value based on how the soil or our plant appears. This will help prevent false alarms for plants that require less water. Second, it also gives us a fast way to turn off the alarm, since we can turn the potentiometer to below even the lowest plant sensor value.

That would be all we need to run our plant alarm. We could add batteries to make it remote, but overall our plant alarm is just want we need to keep on top of watering our plants! The next step is to try to recreate this same program not in blocks, but instead in MicroPython!

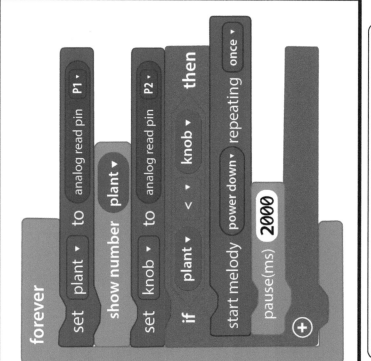

Our plant variable will save the soil conductivity sensor reading we measure on Pin 1

Scroll the value of plant on the LED display

Our knob variable will save the potentiometer measurement we take on Pin 2.

If our plant value is less than our knob value, trigger the power down sound effect to play once.

Pause our program for two seconds (2000 milliseconds) as the sound effect plays to prevent it from playing the effect multiple overlapping times.

You should feel free to change the delay in between the sound effects for a less frequent alarm, or change the sound effect if there is another one you would prefer

Programming in micro:Python

Now that we have already programmed our plant sensor, we are going to retype it in a new programing language: micro:Python! In order to use micro:Python, we have to pick a different code editor, since our makecode only writes in blocks or Javascript. Go to https://python.microbit.org and use the online editor.

You may be asking why you would want to program in a language other than the micro:bit blocks. While all programming languages share similarities, different languages have different specialties or options. Perhaps the functionality you are looking for in your project works better in another language. It never hurts to know a little bit of different programming languages since they can make you better at your primary one as well!

There are a few similarities and differences between the block code and this Python code we just wrote, but overall it will provide the same exact functionality. Click download and then upload your new Python created hex micro:bit code file as you would normally. We have just written our first Python program for the micro:bit, but our last project for the book!

Python needs you to enclose commands by indenting them exactly four spaces, no more, no less. The micro:bit will warn us with a scrolling error if we make a mistake.

```python
from microbit import *
import music
while True:
    plant = pin1.read_analog()
    display.scroll(str(plant))
    knob = pin2.read_analog()
    if plant < knob:
        music.play(music.POWER_DOWN)
        sleep(2000)
```

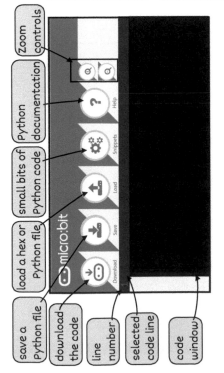

- save a Python file
- download the code
- line number
- selected code line
- code window
- load a hex or Python file
- small bits of Python code
- Python documentation
- Zoom controls

As you can see, it is fairly similar to what we have been working with already, except the coding window is blank! Instead of dragging blocks into our code area, we have to type our program in the Python language. Here is a copy of the same plant alarm program we just wrote in blocks written in Python code.

Advanced suggestions

This book is only the beginning! A few possibilities I thought worth highlighting include:

Programming via bluetooth with a smart phone

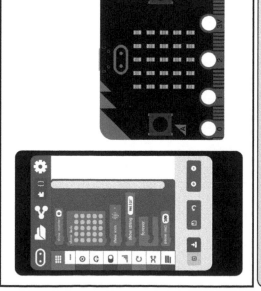

There are smart phone apps which allow you to connect remotely to your micro:bit in order to upload block code. This is helpful if you are building a project away from a computer and want to make small changes, or try something completely new!

Syncing multiple micro:bit

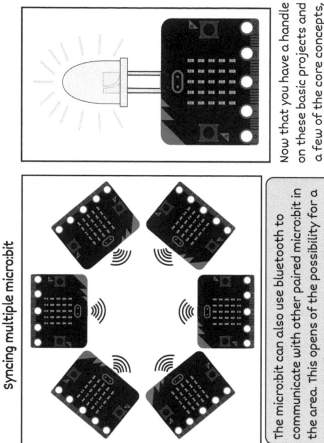

The micro:bit can also use bluetooth to communicate with other paired micro:bit in the area. This opens of the possibility for a large array of sensors in one area, or perhaps a large-scale multiplayer game where each player gets their own micro:bit!

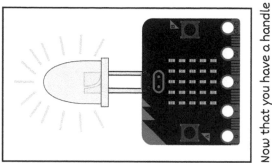

Now that you have a handle on these basic projects and a few of the core concepts, the only limit for what types of projects you build is your imagination!

Parts List

Find these parts online at www.jameco.com

Item	Qty
BBC micro:bit	1
3 foot MicroUSB Cable	1
400-Point Solderless Breadboard	1
Alligator Clips	1
Alligator Clips to Banana Plug (3 Pack)	1
Flexible-wire Jumpers Male to Male	1
2 AA Battery Holder	1
220 Ohn Resistors	30
10 kOhm Resistors	20
Red LEDs	10
Green LEDS	10
Yellow LEDS	10
Mini-DC Fan	2
Tri-color LED	3
Speaker	1
Photoresistors	3
Soil Moisture Sensor	1
IR Emitter	5
IR Collector	5
4-Wheel Robot Cart kit	1
PIR Sensor	1
3.3V Voltage Regulator	1
5 Volt Voltage Regulator	1
L293D 4 channel motor driver	2
HR-SR05 Ultrasonic Distance Sensor	1
Potentiometer	1
Edge Connector Breakout Board for Microbit	1

Find these materials at a local craft store...

Item	Qty
Cardboard	1
Plain baseball cap	1
Foam Tape (1")	1
Hot Glue	1
Clear Tape	1
Thin breathable mesh (for covering fans)	1

Get these most anywhere...

	Qty
AA batteries	4

Downloading code

You can find links to all the code used in this book at
https://gitlab.com/MakerMediaBooks/easy_microbit_projects

Glossary

Accelerometer: a sensor that measures the acceleration of an object

Analog: Any sensor or output which has a variety of possible values.

Array: a data structure used to hold multiple pieces of information which can later be accessed

Boolean: a data type which has two possible values, either True or False.

Conditional statement: a logic-based statement used in programming to determine outcomes

Current: a property of electricity which measures the flow of electrical charge. Electronic components consume current.

Digital: Any sensor or output which is restricted to an ON or OFF position

Extension: also known as a library, any collection of code which contributes additional capabilities to our programming language

Frequency: the number of time something happens per second. Higher frequency tones have a higher ptich.

Index: the location of an item in the array. Index starts at a value of 0 for the first spot in the array.

Input: any sensor value or user interaction

Klaxxon: any noise used to indicate attention; another word for horn.

LED: stands for Light Emitting Diode, a small electronic light

Output: any action produced from our micro:bit, including activating lights, sounds, or motors

Programming Loop: one of any number of programming-based repeated actions. Some continue forever, while others cease once a some condition is met

Pulse Width Modulation: a technique by which digital pins can create analog values by controling the average time a pin is triggered.

Resistance: a property of all materials which determines how well electricity flows through the material

Resistor: an electrical component which helps to control the flow of electricity through a circuit by restricting the flow.

Sensor: any device which takes a reading on the physical world

Serial: A communication protocol which allows our micro:bit to talk to our computer or other devices

Threshold: a value at which an event or function gets activated

True or false: Possible values when evaluating a logic statement or mathematical comparison

Tone: an audio sound created by modulating a soundwave

Variable: a programming concept, using a name to store some amount of information

Voltage: a property of electricity which measures the electromotive force, or potential